STAR TREK™
Cocktails
A Stellar Compendium

Written by **Glenn Dakin**

Art by **Adrian Salmon**

Photographs by **David Burton & Jess Esposito**

Mixology consultants
Simon Pellet, Adrian Calderbank

TITANBOOKS

Contents

"Gi'e us your glass."

Scotty, 'By Any Other Name,'

TOS

Have you tasted a Samarian Sunset? Or blown your taste buds away with a Warp Core Breach? The chances are you have never left planet Earth... But we can dream. Alongside the thrill of discovering the universe, the allure and peril of the world of drink is a thread running through man's attempt to explore the unknown.

"Sometimes a man'll tell his bartender things he'll never tell his doctor." This line, from Dr. Boyce to Captain Pike, is from 'The Cage,' *Star Trek*'s first pilot episode. The martini Boyce makes was the first drink in that futuristic world, and made it very clear that alcohol was not going to be outmoded in the 23rd century. Gene Roddenberry, creator of the show, was full of visionary notions

– a world without prejudice, inequality, poverty or materialism. But the Great Bird of the Galaxy was wise enough to know that a future with no recognizable human behavior would have viewers in the present switching off.

"Sometimes a man'll tell his bartender things he'll never tell his doctor."

At the time the first series was made, drinking was very much part of the social glue. Viewers might accept a future without smoking (*Star Trek* was prophetic in its removal of tobacco from society), but a world of friends, work pals, comrades in arms, without the odd glass together? Hard to imagine.

Star Trek has been called "*Wagon Train* to the stars," after the popular NBC Western of the time, and drink is used in the first series very much as it is used in the Western genre... to start fights, and then... well,

to make up after them.
It is also there for comedy, with
suitably goofy incidental music
to let us know such folly was
not to be taken too seriously.
In the world of drinking, there
were certain unwritten rules.
Anyone with Scottish or Irish
origins was allowed to get seriously
(meaning comically) drunk. In
the episode, 'By Any Other Name,'
Scotty famously helped thwart an

invasion of super-intelligent aliens by drinking one of them under the table. With typical humor, Scotty was also shown to be incapacitated himself.

Drink added to the party atmosphere of possibly the most popular episode of all, 'The Trouble with Tribbles,' helping to lead to a barroom brawl with the Klingons. In this memorable scene, Chekov insisted that Scotch had been invented by a little old lady from Leningrad.

The captain and first officer were more restrained. When Kirk swigged some Saurian Brandy in 'The Enemy Within,' it was to show us the wayward behavior of his evil side, released in a transporter malfunction. It was a characteristic of the level-headed Vulcans that they did not drink alcohol.

The original *Star Trek* series was, like its Western origins, inclined to turn to whisky as its tipple of choice. Scotch or bourbon was the default drink in any 60s TV series, and it required a specific plot-driven reason for any variation. With the arrival of Chekov, vodka joined the drinking menus of the future. The movies added invented dangers like Romulan ale.

In *Star Trek: The Next Generation* Roddenberry ventured even further into the future. Here, there was a terrifying new development... synthehol, introduced in 'Up the Long Ladder.' This was Roddenberry's 'dream ticket' for the future of drink, a computer-created copy of alcohol that left the drinker with no side-effects, namely no hangover.

Synthehol didn't mean that drinking was consigned to the past. In fact, the opposite was true. The *Enterprise*'s replicators can make a perfect martini, and with the introduction of the bar Ten-Forward, drinking became even more established in the fabric of starship life. And, as Scotty discovered, Guinan has a few bottles of the real thing stashed behind the bar.

Especially in its early days, TNG had a relaxed air and the inclusion of the dimly-lit drinking lounge underlined this. It became a venue for deep conversation, intimate moments, a touch of self-analysis. The post-work drink had become an accepted part of starship life, a touch that added to the easy charm of the series.

The curious android Data became an amusing lens through which to study the human relationship with alcohol, and one scene, in *Star Trek: Generations* summed this up nicely. After being fitted with an emotion chip, Data proceeded to try a drink in Ten-Forward, "a little something from Forcas III."

After trying a couple, Data is
quick to conclude, "I hate this!"
"More?" Guinan asks, doubtfully.
"Please!" comes the reply.
Synthehol was commonly used in
Voyager, without the reservations
attached to it in TNG. In fact,
tough old Seven of Nine became
intoxicated on one glass
of synthetic champagne.

"I hate this!" Data exclaims.

"More?" Guinan asks, doubtfully.

The Doctor diagnosed that the
Borg could not hold their liquor.
In this series, the strong drink
preferred by Captain Janeway
was good old black coffee.

Getting together for a post-work
glass or two was more fundamental
to *Deep Space Nine*, where Quark's
Bar was literally at the center of
the promenade. Set on the
fringes of galactic civilization,
DS9 frequently used drink in its
storytelling, a companion suitable
for a frontier life of excess, regret,
rumor, and riot.

Star Trek took a surprise turn,
back in time, for its next series:
Enterprise. As this reflected
the earlier days of space
exploration it was not unusual
to find a bottle of bourbon stowed
away in a shuttlepod, (which
Tucker and Reed did). Again,
alcohol was used to loosen tongues
and bring characters together.

In the recent series, *Discovery*
(once again, set before the
original), drink is part of the crew's
life. 'Magic to Make the Sanest Man
Go Mad' shows a wild party

on board the *U.S.S. Discovery*. Tilly's post-work de-stressing involves bouncing a ping-pong ball into a glass of beer. Such letting down of hair was unheard of in any earlier versions of *Star Trek* and probably says more about the loosening up of the society that made the show, than anything else.

Star Trek: Picard was keen to make the statement that this was a show for grown-ups. Years after Seven of Nine was so vulnerable to mere synthehol, she is fond of "bourbon, straight up." Raffi, Picard's troubled ally, sat at *La Sirena*'s controls while swigging straight from the bottle.

Cocktails themselves have featured in *Star Trek*, and a couple of classics await you here, including the delightful Samarian Sunset from TNG, a drink that changes color at a light 'ping' on the side of the glass. We'll do our best to conjure that, without 24th-century technology.

Also, we present a drink destined to become a classic, the explosive

Warp Core Breach, a cocktail said to be able to relax you for several days afterward, as made by Quark. Alongside classic cocktails with a *Star Trek* twist, we also feature completely new *Trek*-inspired concoctions, that you will be among the first in the Galaxy to taste.

So replicate your ingredients and engage your taste buds. Let's see what's out there...

1

First Contact

(Aperitifs)

Jean-Luc's
Earl Grey Martini

When contemplating your vineyard or possibly the state of galactic politics on the holo-news, this Earl Grey martini will make you feel as sophisticated as Jean-Luc Picard and as chilled out as a retired Starfleet admiral. Picard would certainly admire the careful planning required to prepare your cold Earl Grey tea. If your replicator is on the blink then you will enjoy making use of the real thing: fragrant, loose leaf Earl Grey tea. Taken early in the evening, this refined tipple will soon have you ready to say, "Let's see what's out there..."

2fl oz/50ml gin

1¼fl oz/35ml cold Earl Grey tea

1fl oz/25ml lemon juice

½fl oz/12.5ml sugar syrup

Garnish: a twist of lemon peel

Place ingredients in a mixing glass and stir well.

Strain the liquid into a teacup or martini glass and garnish with lemon.

"Tea, Earl Grey, hot."

Jean-Luc Picard, 'Contagion,' TNG

Live Long
and Prosper

1½fl oz/40ml tequila

Bottle of home-made trixian bubble juice:

2 tbsp/30ml grapefruit juice

2 tsp/10ml raspberry syrup

1½fl oz/40ml soda water

As refreshing as the spring winds on Mount Seleya, this delicious cocktail combines a discreet level of alcohol with a healthy measure of grapefruit juice. While it is not logical to drink to excess, Vulcans do partake of wine and other stronger beverages when it is culturally appropriate. This long drink provides an elegant ratio of water to alcohol which is also pleasing to the mathematical mind. Be sure to serve with the ancient Vulcan salute.

Fill a highball or other tall glass with ice, combine the ingredients and stir well.

"You're welcome, I believe is the correct response."

Mr. Spock, 'Bread and Circuses,' TOS

"All hands, brace for impact!"

Jean-Luc Picard, *Star Trek: Nemesis*

Set Chasers
to Stun

1fl oz/25ml lemon juice

½fl oz/12.5ml orange curaçao

½fl oz/12.5ml lime juice

1⅓fl oz/37.5ml Grand Marnier

2 tsp/10ml grenadine (six dashes)

A bright, cheerful drink to help along any first contact scenario, this fruity cocktail blends the orange flavors of Grand Marnier and curaçao with grenadine and lemon. Just as a versatile phaser can be set to disintegrate or merely stun, this cocktail can be modulated to simply warm the heart or blast your blues away. After this drink you will certainly stun your first contact with your relaxed, happy vibes and a second contact will not seem light years away.

Fill a cocktail shaker with ice, add the ingredients and shake well. Strain into a champagne glass or cocktail glass.

Chekov's
Uncle Vanya

Chekov is devoted to all things Russian, so he is sure to approve of this tall, sweet, vodka-based cocktail. He would be proud that it is named after a play by his writer namesake, Anton Chekhov. To cap it all, the star of this production is the blackberry and, since Russia is one of the world's greatest berry producers, even the liqueur could be from his homeland. Sipping this, Chekov would be in paradise... which he assures us is a place just outside of Moscow.

2fl oz/50ml vodka

1 fl oz/25ml blackberry liqueur

1 fl oz/25ml lemon juice (preferably fresh)

2 tsp/10ml gomme syrup (a simple syrup with gum arabic)

Ice

2 blackberries or handful of blueberries

Garnish: 1 lemon wheel

Load a cocktail shaker with ice, add the ingredients, including the berries, and muddle. Double strain into a Collins glass, already loaded with ice. Add more berries and stir a little to spread them around the glass.
Garnish with lemon.

"Scotch? It was invented by
a little old lady from Leningrad."

Chekov, 'The Trouble with Tribbles,' TOS

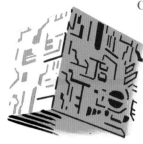

Borg Queen

Say goodbye to your weak human side and take back control with this chilling variation of the martini. The Borg Queen has a subtle edge on the classic martini, with the addition of pineapple. Or if you're ready to assimilate something a bit more mouth-tingling, a dash of lemon juice. It was once said that the martini was the one perfect invention America had given the world, and the Borg seek perfection in all things. So add a couple of Borg ice cubes and lower your shields. Resistance is futile.

½in/1cm slice of pineapple, crushed

1 tbsp/15ml sweet vermouth

1 tbsp/15ml extra dry vermouth

1¼fl oz/35ml gin

Ice

Optional: dash of lemon juice

Garnish: pineapple leaf or quarter slice

Muddle the pineapple in a cocktail shaker. Add ingredients and ice. Shake well and strain into a cocktail glass. Garnish with pineapple leaf, or a quarter slice on the rim.

"Resistance is futile."

The Borg, 'The Best of Both Worlds,' TNG

By Any
Other Name

A powerful alien who has taken human
form (and is not used to it) suffers when
Scotty introduces him to Scotch.

[Scott's quarters]
(The last drops of Scotch
go into Tomar's glass.)

Tomar: Very interesting. But I feel
rather strange. (He makes some
jerking motions then falls off his
chair onto the floor.)

Scott: We did it, you and me.
Put him right under the table.
(He takes the paralyzer off Tomar's
belt) I'll take this to the captain.

(He gets to the door, then stops
and gently falls back against
the wall. He slides to the floor,
as out of it as Tomar is)

2

Shore Leave

(Cocktails for Chilling)

Sulu's

San Francisco

Hailing from San Francisco, Sulu cannot resist a taste of home when it's cocktail hour and he's thousands of light years from Earth. Of course, the San Francisco of the 23rd century is a little different from our own, with Starfleet HQ gleaming on the skyline, but that just makes this drink even more appropriate for a proud captain who has served on many starships. A keen botanist, Sulu will enjoy the exotic array of plant flavors that blend in the bitters of this tall sweet drink. He might even spear a cherry with a cocktail cutlass after a hard workout fencing.

1fl oz/25ml sloe gin

1fl oz/25ml dry vermouth

1fl oz/25ml sweet vermouth

Peychaud's bitters (a dash)

Angostura bitters (a dash)

Ice

Garnish: Amarena or maraschino cherry

Fill a shaker with ice and add the ingredients. Shake well as if the ship were under attack and shields at 20%. Strain into a cocktail glass and garnish.

"Just what the doctor ordered."

Sulu, 'Shore Leave,' TOS

Guinan
Fizz

The barkeeper at Ten-Forward knows just what her customers need. Guinan comes from a race of listeners and from the slightest word of her regulars, knows whether to serve this classic fizz Tom Collins-style, with sweeter gin and ice, or classic gin fizz-style, a shade more bitter. For garnish, mint or cucumber provide that summer feeling – with a dash of cosmic wisdom on the side.

2 fl oz/50ml gin

1fl oz/25ml lemon juice

½fl oz/12.5ml gomme syrup

Cucumber slices

Sparkling water (to top)

Ice

Garnish: a slice of lemon or cucumber and mint

Mix the gin, lemon juice, syrup, and a few slices of cucumber into a cocktail shaker and pack with ice cubes. Shake intensely with a profound look of Guinan-like mystery on your face. Strain and pour into a tall glass which you have already filled with ice. Finish with sparkling water and decorate with the lemon slice or cucumber and mint.

"I tend bar, and I listen."

Guinan, 'Ensign Ro,' TNG

Spock's Slipper

As green as the blood of a Vulcan, this drink is perfect for sharing a Spock-like moment of contemplation on your favorite holiday world. It would perhaps meet with Mr. Spock's approval, as the bright green Midori generally has half the alcohol content of many cocktail mainstays, such as the bourbon in Dr. McCoy's Mint Julep. A sweet liqueur, Midori, which means 'green' in Japanese, works well melded with lemon juice to create the perfect Vulcan balance. For a warm spring or summer day – on a Class-M planet – it's the logical choice.

2 fl oz/50ml tequila

1fl oz/25ml Midori (melon liqueur)

1fl oz/25ml lime juice

Ice

Garnish: melon ball or maraschino cherry

Fill a cocktail shaker with ice and add the ingredients. Shake well. Place a bed of crushed ice in a martini glass and pour the drink on top. Add the melon ball or cherry.

"Fascinating."

Spock, 'The City on the Edge of Forever,' TOS

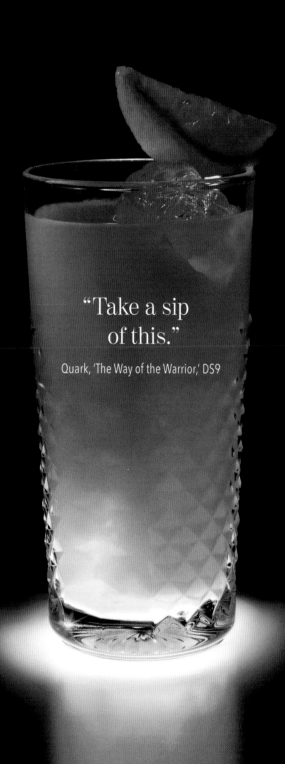

"Take a sip
of this."

Quark, 'The Way of the Warrior,' DS9

Ferengi
Wallbanger

2fl oz/50ml vodka

Orange juice, to top up

1 tbsp/15ml green chartreuse

2 tbsp/30ml Galliano

Cherry

Ice

Garnish: orange slice

Bring yourself all the joy of happy hour at Quark's Bar with this potent Ferengi potion. As the weather is always bad on the Ferengi homeworld (they have 178 words for rain) they need can't-fail fun drinks to blow away the blues. The Ferengi like a good trade, and are happy to exchange an evening of partying for a hangover. Be careful when drinking with Ferengi, after a couple of drinks they may wish to exchange 'Oo-Mox' – a sensual ear massage. Just saying.

Put the cherry into a highball glass, then build an ice 'stair' to the top. Pour in the vodka, then add the orange juice almost to fill. With the artistry of Quark, gently add the chartreuse, then the Galliano to the top of the 'stair' so they make a layer on the surface. Decorate with your orange slice.

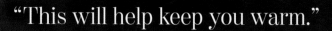

"This will help keep you warm."

Martia, *Star Trek VI: The Undiscovered Country*

Ice

Planet

1¼fl oz/35ml white rum

4 tsp/20ml blue curaçao

4 tsp/20ml lime juice

1 tbsp/15ml gomme syrup

4 tsp/20ml lemonade

Ice

This ice spectacular will chill you out on even the most sultry evening. The Klingon prison world of Rura Penthe – known as the alien's graveyard – is the perfect place to get away from it all, and this drink will take you there. Just as the frozen surface of the asteroid conceals precious dilithium crystals, this creation conceals a precious heart of blue curaçao. Add a sizzling top-up of lemonade for that special atmospheric touch...

Combine the first four ingredients in a blender with ice. Pour into a highball glass and pour the lemonade on top for the atmospheric effect. No garnish needed – you are in prison, human!

This Side of Paradise

On a paradise planet, Dr. McCoy makes a Mint Julep for Kirk...

MCCOY: Sho'nuf. Hey, Jim boy, y'all ever have a real cold Georgia-style mint julep, huh?

KIRK: Look, Bones, I need your help. Can you run tests, blood samples, anything at all to give us a lead on what these things are, how to counteract them?

MCCOY: Who wants to counteract paradise, Jim boy?

3

Holodeck Honeymoon

(Romantic)

Q-Pid

4 tsp/20ml vodka

1½fl oz/40ml cherry liqueur

Egg white

Ice

Garnish: raspberry powder

Q may be a godlike being from an extra-dimensional plane of existence, but all matters human have a certain charm for him. Perhaps our follies reveal us the most, and in the realm of love what follies are beyond us? Q once tested Picard's capacity for love, and this cocktail will get you in the mood to explore its mystery too. Cupid-styled drinks come in as many forms as Q has costume changes, so there are many chances to fall in love with this cocktail.

> "This human emotion, love, is a dangerous thing..."
>
> Q, 'Q-Pid,' TNG

Combine the ingredients in a cocktail shaker and dry shake (without ice). Then wet shake (with ice). This will produce a better foam. Pour into a coupe or traditional cocktail glass. For garnish, draw a heart or flower (or Starfleet delta) on top with raspberry powder.

Worf's
Smooth Move

Most Klingons need a stiff drink sometimes, especially when romance is in the air. The rum in this drink evokes the spirit of adventure, and the prune juice speaks to the warrior in all of us. Prunes have many beneficial properties, and also help you to keep regular, among the highly irregular challenges of space. Garnish with a pineapple spear, if you find it too hard to carve a pineapple *bat'leth*.

Combine the ingredients in a shaker with ice. Muddle the fresh ginger also, to taste – it can have quite a kick. Serve with a pineapple spear (or *bat'leth*) in a parfait-style glass. For extra romance, coat the glass rim with sugar by running a lime wedge around it and dipping (before you put the drink in, of course.)

1 fl oz/25ml white rum

2 fl oz/50ml pineapple juice

2 fl oz/50ml prune juice

1 tbsp/15ml lemon juice

1 tbsp/15ml lime juice

1 fl oz/25ml gomme syrup

Several slices of fresh ginger

Ice

Garnish: spear of pineapple

"A warrior's drink."

Worf, 'Yesterday's Enterprise,' TNG

"Our minds,
sharing the same
thoughts."

Spock, 'Dagger of the Mind,' TOS

Mind-Meld

2 tbsp/30ml vodka

2–2½fl oz/50–70ml champagne

2 tsp/10ml cherry liqueur

2 tsp/10ml lemon juice

2 tsp/10ml flower syrup (rose, hibiscus or elderflower...)

Ice

Garnish: 6–8 raspberries and/or edible flowers

The Vulcans may not be famous for their romantic side, but they do know a lot about two becoming one, as the ancient art of the mind-meld shows. You don't have to study Vulcan mysticism, or even place your fingers on someone's face to experience the shared joy of this cosmically consensual cocktail. A dash of flower syrup will add to the mind-blowing effect. Within logical parameters, of course. Perfect for smoothing out that lovers' tiff, and bringing minds – and hearts – back together.

Put everything in a shaker with ice and shake. Pour into a huge wine glass and top it up with champagne (2–2½fl oz/ 50–70ml). Garnish with berries or edible flowers on top. Drink romantically with two straws.

Heaven
of Nine

This elegant, distinctive cocktail is as cool and impressive as the Borg-enhanced Seven of Nine. Like the sometime *Voyager* crew member and Fenris Ranger, this concoction commands respect and is bound to make an impression when ordered on a first date. Based on the classic White Lady, a favorite drink of spies and detectives, it has a certain mystique that goes well with the enigmatic Seven. After a tough day working for the collective, you are bound to rediscover your human side after one of these and realize that where romance is concerned, resistance is useless.

1¾fl oz/45ml gin

1 tbsp/15ml Cointreau (orange liqueur)

1 tbsp/15ml lemon juice

1 egg white

Ice

Garnish: lemon or grapefruit peel.

Place all the ingredients in a shaker with ice. Shake well and serve in a cocktail glass. Garnish with peel.

"Fun will now commence."

Seven of Nine, 'Ashes to Ashes,' VOY

Par'Mach

on the Beach

Even Klingons are sometimes in search of love, although not of the tender kind. This cocktail, with its warrior-strength combination of vodka and peach schnapps, will give any Klingon the courage to seek out a suitably fiery partner. Based on the Earth potion 'Sex on the Beach,' its name evokes not just the joys of *par'Mach*, but also the sensual delight of this most luscious of drinks. *par'Mach* has been known to leave its participants in need of hospital care, so be prepared for an emergency medical pick-me-up after having too many of these.

3fl oz/80ml cranberry juice

3fl oz/80ml of pineapple juice

1½fl oz/40ml peach schnapps

1½fl oz/40ml cherry liqueur

2¼fl oz/60ml vodka

2 tbsp/30ml lemon juice

Ice

Garnish: cocktail cherries, orange slice, sprig of mint

Load two highball glasses with ice. Mix all the ingredients in a shaker, or stir in a jug with ice, then pour. Garnish with cocktail cherries, and/or an orange slice and sprig of mint.

"*Par'Mach* is the Klingon word for love, but with more aggressive overtones."

Dax, 'Looking for *par'Mach* in All the Wrong Places,' DS9

Star Trek Generations

★

Data learns to like drinking, with Geordi and Guinan.

GUINAN: Gentlemen, something new from Forcas III.

(She pours two glasses, Data takes a drink)

LA FORGE: What?

DATA: I believe this beverage has provoked an emotional response.

LA FORGE: Really? What do you feel?

DATA: I am uncertain. Because I have had little experience with emotion I am unable to ...articulate the sensation.

GUINAN: Emotion?

LA FORGE: I'll explain later.

DATA: Ouf!

GUINAN: It looks like he hates it.

DATA: Yes. That is it. I hate this.

LA FORGE: Data, I think the chip is working.

DATA: Yes. I hate this! It is revolting!

GUINAN: More?

DATA: Please.

4

Journey
to Babel

(Entertaining)

23rd-Century Manhattan

Enjoy the sophistication of 23rd-century life with the ultimate stylish cocktail, the classic Manhattan. The city of the future is a place of white spires and quiet shuttlecraft gliding across a clear blue sky – and the serenity of mankind's warp age can be yours to enjoy with this timeless drink. Manhattan has produced a few surprises for the *Star Trek* crews over the years – Nazi invasion, time-travel paradoxes, alien interference... but there will be no surprises with this perfect beverage, just quintessential big city pleasure.

2fl oz/50ml rye whiskey or bourbon

1fl oz/25ml sweet vermouth

Angostura bitters – two dashes

Plum or rhubarb bitters – optional dash

Garnish: a couple of maraschino cherries

Combine the drink ingredients in a chilled coupe or martini glass and stir. Garnish with the cherries.

"I think I'm going to like this century."

Kirk, 'The City on the Edge of Forever,' TOS

T'Pol's Vulcan Grasshopper

This delightful after-dinner concoction captures the mystery at the heart of the Vulcan race. Many make the mistake of thinking that Vulcans have no feelings. The truth is that they have such deep feelings they are forced to subdue them, or be overwhelmed, as Commander T'Pol of the *Enterprise NX-01* has revealed. The Vulcan Grasshopper cocktail embodies that paradox, as its bright green alien look and ice-cold exterior conceal much to delight. So sweet and delicious, it would be truly illogical to share.

2 tbsp/30ml crème de menthe

2 tbsp/30ml white crème de cacao

2 tbsp/30ml light/single cream

Ice

Garnish: mint sprig, dark chocolate sprinkles

Combine the ingredients in a shaker, about half filled with ice, then strain into a cocktail or coupe glass and garnish. Note: This drink can also be made in a blender, for a more dessert-like effect.

"There's no need to be restrained by human morality."

T'Pol, 'Bounty,' ENT

"They were once considered mortal enemies of the Klingon Empire."

Worf, 'Trials and Tribble-ations,' DS9

To Bibble

With Tribbles

2 tbsp/30ml Irish Cream

1½fl oz/40ml bourbon or rye whiskey

4 tsp/20ml coffee liqueur

2 tsp/10ml hazelnut syrup

Garnish: Marshmallows, chocolate or cinnamon powder to taste

What could be better than a tribble-related cocktail? Two tribble bibulations, of course! The crew of Deep Space 9 traveled back in time to be surrounded by warm fuzzy tribbles, due to a temporal anomaly (No, that's not another cocktail!), and you too can get that fuzzy feeling by concocting this most treaty of drinks. Your tribbles will be made of marshmallows, and if you're Klingon you might want to toast them first for extra satisfaction. The warm glow comes from the Irish Cream.

Mix the ingredients in a shaker, then pour into a rocks glass. For the garnish, place an absinthe spoon on the cup with a few small, burnt marshmallows – with chocolate or cinnamon powder – to remind you of those cute little tribbles.

Odo's

Chameleon

2 tbsp/30ml vodka

4 tsp/20ml elderflower liqueur

2 tsp/10ml lime juice

1 tsp/5ml green melon liqueur

2 tsp/10ml grenadine

4 tsp/20ml orange juice

As a Changeling, Odo is sure to appreciate the morphing qualities of this show-stopping cocktail, which adds entertainment to drinking pleasure. Mix up your vodka base, and just when your guests think they know what to expect, add the green melon liqueur for the chameleon effect. To change it into a Veiled Chameleon just add the grenadine. As a dedicated follower of the rules, Odo will never agree to serving it in any old cocktail glass – a wine glass is preferred. But he will appreciate its liquid charms – after all, deep down he is a fluid, shapeless mass himself.

"Well, another satisfied customer."

Odo, 'Babel,' DS9

Combine the vodka, elderflower, and lime in a shaker, then strain into a wine glass. Add the green melon liqueur, grenadine, and orange juice in that order for the chameleon effect. Stir and enjoy.

Captain Janeway's

Irish Coffee

When the perfect dinner party comes to an end, you can't make a guest feel more at home than by offering them an Irish Coffee. Janeway's love of the hot black stuff is legendary. She has been known to have four cups in the morning and claims coffee helped her beat the Borg. It takes patience and fine judgment to bring a starship back home across the Delta Quadrant, qualities also required to pour the thick cream slowly over the back of a spoon and top this drink to perfection.

4 tsp/20ml heavy/double cream

4½fl oz/120ml black filter coffee

2fl oz/50ml Irish whiskey

1 tbsp brown sugar, or 2 tsp/10ml sugar syrup to taste. Or try hazelnut or vanilla syrup.

Prepare the cream separately: whip to thicken slightly. Pour the coffee into an Irish Coffee glass and add the whiskey and sugar. Pour cream over the back of a spoon to layer onto the coffee. Sit back and reminisce about your time in the Delta Quadrant.

"Coffee – the finest organic
suspension ever devised."

Janeway, 'Hunters,' VOY

Someone To Watch Over Me

On *Voyager*, the Doctor teaches Seven of Nine some human social rituals...

EMH: Seven, perhaps now would be a good time to review lesson twenty-three, Toast of the Town.

SEVEN: Very well.

(She goes to the middle of the room and taps her glass.)

SEVEN: Ladies and gentlemen,
I require your attention.
May cultural differences encourage
us to build bridges of understanding.
To all that makes us unique.

(Applause)

69

5

Neelix's Celebration Cocktails

(Party Time!)

"A few sips of this...
and you'll be relaxed for
the next three days."

Quark, 'His Way,' DS9

Warp Core
Breach

For 2

1½fl oz/40ml white rum

2 tbsp/30ml spiced rum

1½fl oz/40ml dark rum

2 tbsp/30ml cointreau

1½fl oz/40ml lime juice

3fl oz/80ml guava juice

2fl oz/50ml cranberry juice

1½fl oz/40ml strawberry juice

Crushed ice

Make your party go with a *Kaboom* with this unforgettable treat. On a starship, just about the worst thing that could happen (apart from drinking one of Neelix's cocktails before breakfast) is a warp core breach. In such a catastrophe, matter and anti-matter collide explosively. In this cocktail, rum and fruit flavors collide to similar effect. It's worth making extra effort with your replicator to create the smoking effect, for full theatrical impact. Perfect for sharing with like-minded deep space travelers.

Combine all the ingredients in your shaker and mix well. Load a bowl with crushed ice. Pour the mixture into the bowl to share. For the smoke effect, use a cinnamon stick. Light one end and the smoke will come from the other. Or use a smoke machine if you have one.

Buck's
Fizzbin

Any day of celebration gets off to an effervescent start with a refreshing glass of orange juice and champagne. This drink will bring as much sparkle into your life as a convivial hand of fizzbin, the card game played on Beta Antares IV (or so Kirk claimed). Like the game, the rules of Buck's Fizzbin are eccentric, so you might wish to replace one measure of champagne with grenadine for a half-fizzbin (if it's a Tuesday) or include a dash of vodka for a 'Ferengi Wallbanger Fizzbin,' if fizzbinning at night. For a classic Royal Fizzbin, add a little cherry liqueur, as human kings and queens did way back in the 21st century.

3½fl oz/100 ml fresh orange juice

7fl oz/200 ml chilled champagne

Garnish: orange slice

Pour half the OJ into two champagne flutes. Top up with champagne. It's that simple. (Unlike Fizzbin).

"The name of the game is called, uh... fizzbin."

Kirk, 'A Piece of the Action,' TOS

Fuzzy
Tribble

Everybody loves a tribble – unless you're a Klingon – and this drink brings you all the joy of a space station packed with the furry balls of fun. It is said the tribble's purr has a tranquilizing effect on the human brain, and this cocktail with its delicious dose of peach schnapps will do the same – without taking over your entire home. If you want a hairier tribble simply add a little more vodka to the mix, and very soon all your tribbles will be far away.

1fl oz/25ml vodka

1fl oz/25ml peach schnapps

2fl oz/50ml orange juice

1 tbsp/15ml lime juice

Garnish: slice of orange

Simply load a highball glass with ice and pour over the vodka and schnapps, then the juice. Stir and serve with a slice of orange.

"Can I interest you in a harmless tribble?"

Cyrano Jones, 'The Trouble with Tribbles,' TOS

"Find something you love,
then do it the best you can."

Sisko, 'Shadowplay,' DS9

Sisko's

Sazerac

1fl oz/25ml rye whiskey

1fl oz/25ml cognac

Peychaud's bitters
(2 dashes)

Angostura bitters (1 dash)

Absinthe – a drop or two
to rinse the glass

White sugar cube

Ice

Garnish: twist of lemon
peel

The Sazerac is a real captain's cocktail, a stiff drink to lighten the load of responsibility. Its combination of the mystique of absinthe and the fire of rye whiskey will warm your heart even in the coldest void. Sazerac is the official cocktail of Sisko's hometown of New Orleans, where Sazerac whiskey also originated.
The cocktail has always been a favorite at his father's restaurant, The Creole Kitchen.

Take a mixing glass and muddle a sugar cube with a dash of water. Muddle well, to avoid bits in the drink. (Or use 1 tsp/5ml of sugar syrup). Add the ice, whiskey and bitters. Line another, chilled glass, with the absinthe by running the drops around inside. Pour the first glass into the absinthe-coated glass. Serve with the lemon twist, but then discard the twist.

Tilly's

Ping Pong Beer

Ensign Sylvia Tilly of the *U.S.S. Discovery* admits to being socially awkward, so a game of beer pong helps her relax and make friends. A beer cocktail to match her big personality is the Michelada. Originating from Mexico it adds a spicy kick to your beer with a hit of lime, salt, and cayenne pepper. If you are ready to brave the unknown, there is a wild variation with tomato and clam juice. Tilly would approve your sense of adventure, and it may improve your game of beer pong!

Bottle of Mexican beer to your taste

Cayenne pepper or chili salt

Sea salt

2 ½ limes

Couple of dashes of Mexican Tabasco

1 tsp/5ml Worcestershire sauce (optional)

Ice

Rub your half lime around the rim of the beer glass. Dip the rim in the chili salt to coat. Add the juice of two limes, Tabasco, and Worcestershire sauce to the glass. Add a pinch of sea salt and some ice. Then pour in your beer!

"What the heck...
heck... hell?"

Tilly, 'Despite Yourself,' DSC

Yesterday's Enterprise

In Ten-Forward, Guinan seeks
to give Worf some romantic advice,
and broaden his horizons...

GUINAN: All right. Try this.

WORF: What is it?

GUINAN: Just try it.

(He does, and his face lights up)

GUINAN: You see? It's an Earth
drink. Prune juice.

WORF: A warrior's drink.

6

^

Emergency
Medical
Cocktails

(Relax and Recover)

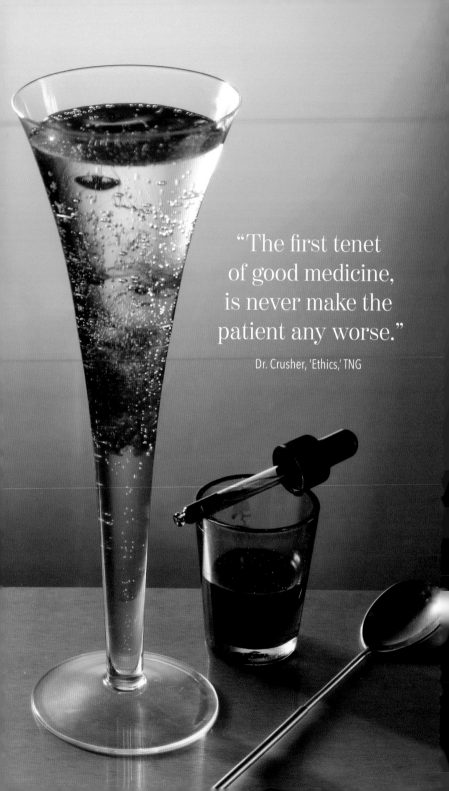

"The first tenet
of good medicine,
is never make the
patient any worse."

Dr. Crusher, 'Ethics,' TNG

Beverly's
Bone Crusher

1 tbsp/15ml white rum

1 tbsp/15ml vodka

1 tbsp/15ml gin

1 tbsp/15ml triple sec

1½ tsp/7.5ml grenadine

1½ tsp/7.5ml lime cordial

1fl oz/25ml champagne
(held back)

Ice

Dash of lemon juice
(optional)

Sticks and stones may break your bones, but Dr. Beverly will be there to restore a 24th-century feeling of wellbeing with her Bone Crusher cocktail. Its rosy glow of health (from the grenadine) conceals the kick of three white liquors: vodka, gin, and white rum. If your sickbay doesn't run to champagne, you can substitute prosecco with no damage to your Hippocratic oath.

Mix all the ingredients (minus champagne) in a shaker, and shake well. Add ice to a tall glass, then pour in the champagne. You could make an ice stair if you are feeling creative. Then add the shaken ingredients. Add an optional dash of lemon to taste. For less serious cases, prescribe lemonade instead of champagne.

Kirk's

Old Fashioned

Captain James T. Kirk is proud of his origins. When once asked if he is from outer space, he proudly says, "No, I'm from Iowa. I only work in outer space." Iowa is the state Templeton Rye comes from, the perfect whiskey to make an Old Fashioned – a cocktail which is said to have medicinal origins. Now, Kirk likes to explore but even he wouldn't mess with this classic, which has been described as the most popular cocktail ever. If you do try the brandy version, make sure it's Saurian Brandy made by the reptile people of the planet Sauria. If not, stick to the original.

2fl oz/50ml rye whiskey (if not available, try bourbon)

Angostura bitters – 2 dashes

1 sugar cube

Soda

Ice

Garnish: twist of orange

In an Old Fashioned glass, muddle a sugar cube with the bitters, a little of the whiskey, and a drop of soda. Add ice, then the whiskey, and garnish with an orange twist on the rim.

"Beauty ... survives."

Kirk, 'That Which Survives,' TOS

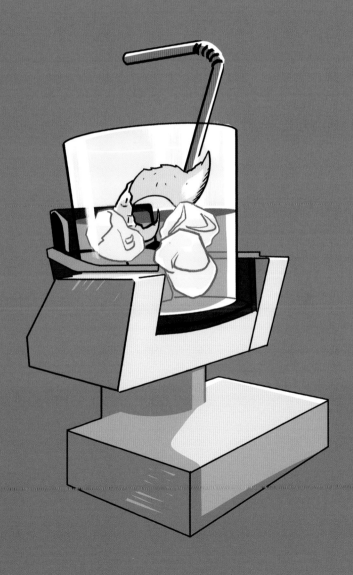

The Lime
Directive

Starfleet General Order 1 insists that starships do not interfere with the alien cultures they discover. In the world of cocktails, there are some things you don't interfere with either, and one is the classic gimlet, a blend of gin and lime cordial. This immortal beverage, beloved of private eyes like Philip Marlowe and Dixon Hill, has medical origins. Lime was added to a navy man's grog to stave off scurvy, and gin was once used to relieve sufferers from tropical ailments. If you wish to break the Lime Directive you can try it with vodka. But don't tell Starfleet.

2fl oz/50ml gin

1fl oz/25ml lime juice

1fl oz/25ml lime cordial

Ice

Garnish: lemon peel cut into a Starfleet delta shape

Mix the ingredients in a cocktail shaker or tall glass with ice. Shake or stir well until very cold. Strain into a chilled coupe glass. Garnish with your lemon delta.

"The Prime Directive
is not just a set of rules;
it is a philosophy."

Picard, 'Symbiosis,' TNG

"Y'all ever have a real cold Georgia style Mint Julep?"

Dr. McCoy, 'This Side of Paradise,' TOS

McCoy's
Mint Julep

2fl oz/50ml bourbon

1½ tsp/7.5ml simple syrup

7-8 mint leaves

Ice

Mint, cardamom, or
classic bitters (optional)

Garnish: mint sprigs

When Dr. McCoy believes he has ended up in paradise on the planet Omicron Ceti III, the only drink he considers worthy of the place is the classic Georgia-style Mint Julep. And it has to be real cold, so pack it with crushed ice. This is Bones' drink of choice to chill out Captain Kirk, who never was much at home in paradise. Now don't forget those tall sprigs coming out the top for the full aromatic sensation... even if on Omicron Ceti III it was alien mint, of course.

Crush the mint leaves well, then add syrup and bourbon in a rocks glass (if you don't have a Julep glass like Bones). Fill half the glass with crushed ice. Give a good stir, pack in more ice, then decorate with mint sprigs. You could also add a dash of mint, cardamom, or classic bitters.

Uhura's

'Distress Call' Dawa

Fluent as she is in Swahili, Lieutenant Uhura knows that the word *dawa* means 'medicine,' and this cocktail is a perfect remedy for low spirits. Monitoring communications at all times, Uhura knows a distress call when she hears it, and Kenya's number one cocktail is the ideal reply to any call for help of the liquid kind. Uhura once said that if she heard the word 'frequency' one more time she would cry, and this cocktail is ideal for anyone who's had a hard day communicating with the universe around them.

2fl oz/50ml vodka

1 tsp white sugar or 1 tbsp brown sugar

1 tbsp honey melted in a little hot water.

2 lime slices

Crushed ice

Put the lime slices in a rocks glass with the sugar. Muddle a little, then add the ice and vodka. Add your honey, melted in a little hot water.

"This isn't reality. This is fantasy."

Uhura, *Star Trek III: The Search for Spock*

His

Way

★

On Deep Space 9, Quark seeks
to find the perfect remedy to cure
the apparent insomnia of Dr. Bashir...

QUARK: You're up late, Doctor.

BASHIR: Yeah, can't sleep.
Feeling a bit tense, actually.

QUARK: I've got just the thing.
One Warp Core Breach coming
right up.

(He puts dry ice into a goldfish
bowl, followed by colored liquids.)

QUARK: A few sips of this and
you'll be relaxed for the next
three days.

7

From Vic
Fontaine With
Love

(Lonely Nights)

"...the great unknown,
beckoning to us."

Dr. Bashir, 'The Quickening,' DS9

Bashir's

London Fog

2fl oz/50ml gin

2 tsp/10ml Pernod or pastis

Ice

Garnish: burnt thyme sprigs (wooden tweezers and lighter needed for this)

This is a drink of misty mystery to lose yourself in, if alone and blue, and Miles O'Brien isn't around for a game of darts. Dr Bashir would appreciate the nod to his British heritage, and his ancestor, the 15th-century poet, Singh el Bashir, would approve of its hidden depths. Counterintuitively, if taken as a morning-after remedy, this cocktail promises to remove the fog from your mind.

Mix the ingredients in your shaker, and pour into a chilled lowball glass, with plenty of crushed or shaved ice. It can also be made in the glass and stirred. Add a twist of lemon to serve. For extra London-weather effect, make with chilled water instead of ice. For a fancy touch, burn some thyme as a garnish and place on the side of the glass.

Scotty's
Rusty Nail

If anyone in the universe knows their drink it should surely be Lieutenant Commander Montgomery Scott, the *Enterprise's* Chief Engineer. This cocktail, favorite of the serious drinker, would meet with his technical approval. It contains nothing but liquor, combining good quality Scotch with sweet, honeyed Drambuie. So before you knock it back, make sure your engines can take it. Aye, laddie, after a couple of these you'll believe you can change the laws of physics...

2fl oz/50ml Scotch whisky

4 tsp/20ml Drambuie

Ice

Garnish: twist of orange peel

Combine the ingredients in a mixing glass, then serve in an Old Fashioned glass with a twist of orange peel to garnish.

"We did it, you and me.
Put him right under the table!"

Scotty, 'By Any Other Name,' TOS

White
Romulan

The Romulan cloaking device famously conceals the arrival of their starships, and this drink will help any fallen warrior to hide their feelings and arm themselves for future battle. Perfect for any of us who have made a failed venture across the Neutral Zone, and need to lick our wounds. The White Romulan is not unlike the White Russian, the manly embrace of the vodka and coffee liqueur with the comforting influence of the cream.

1¼fl oz/35ml vodka

1¼fl oz/35ml Kahlúa or other coffee liqueur

2½fl oz/70ml heavy/ double cream

Garnish: grated nutmeg

Pour the vodka and Kahlúa into an Old Fashioned glass, with ice. Pour the cream on top and give a firm Romulan stir. Add grated nutmeg if desired.

"Glorious. Glorious."

Decius, 'Balance of Terror,' TOS

The Grog
of Khan

If ever you feel abandoned by the one you love or marooned on a lonely world where no one understands you, it's time to channel the fighting spirit of Khan Noonien Singh, the genetically enhanced human tyrant, who was left on Ceti Alpha V. This stiffener of the sinews is based on Navy Grog, and the generous rum will provide a restorative 'Genesis effect' of your very own. Augment with grapefruit juice and lime, and remember that, like revenge, this drink is best served cold.

1fl oz/25ml demerara rum

1fl oz/25ml dark Jamaican rum

1fl oz/25ml white rum

1fl oz/25ml honey mix (honey and water in equal parts)

1 tbsp/15ml lime juice

1 tbsp/15ml grapefruit juice

¾ fl oz/20ml soda

Garnish: slice of lime or slice of orange pierced with cloves

Combine the ingredients in a shaker and strain into a glass with ice. It's best served in a rocks or lowball glass with a wheel of lime. Try as garnish a slice of orange pierced with 2 or 3 cloves. For the full Genesis effect, serve with a cone of ice.

"Best served cold."

Khan, *Star Trek II: The Wrath of Khan*

Klingon
Bird-of-Prey

2 tbsp/30ml gin

4 tsp/20ml green chartreuse

2 tsp/10ml lime juice

2 tsp/10ml Bénédictine

Optional 1–2 tsp/5–10ml tonic water

When all the universe seems against you (and frankly, if you're a Klingon it usually is), you need something with warp capability to take you away from your troubles. This cocktail, like the starship it is named after, is armed and ready to outgun any attack of the blues it encounters. The special warrior's dose of green chartreuse will act like a disruptor cannon and blow your gloom away. As the Klingons say, 'Today is a good day to drink.' Or something very similar.

Combine ingredients in a mixing glass and stir. Pour into a cocktail glass. Add 5–10ml of tonic water, if human.

"Get off your knees and soar."

Korris, 'Heart of Glory,' TNG

The Cage

Captain Pike asks his doctor for a diagnosis on his crew...

BOYCE [OC]: Boyce here.

PIKE: Drop by my cabin, Doctor. **(Boyce enters with bag)** What's that?

I didn't say there's anything wrong with me.

BOYCE: I understand we picked up a distress signal.

PIKE: That's right. Unless we get anything more positive on it, it seems to me the condition of our own crew takes precedent. I'd like to log the ship's doctor's opinion, too.

BOYCE: Oh, I concur with yours, definitely.

PIKE: Good. I'm glad you do, because we're going to stop first at the Vega Colony and replace anybody who needs hospitalization and also. What the devil are you putting in there? Ice?

BOYCE: Who wants a warm martini?

PIKE: What makes you think I need one?

BOYCE: Sometimes a man'll tell his bartender things he'll never tell his doctor. What's been on your mind, Chris, the fight on Rigel VII?

8

Risan Sunset

(After Hours)

Riker's
Midnight Sun

In Alaska, in summertime, the evenings go on forever, which leaves plenty of time for sipping cocktails. Will Riker grew up there, and this cocktail takes him back home. It can take you there too, with just a sip. To capture the glow of that midnight sun, use the sweet warmth of grenadine or cherry brandy. Taking the time to shake and strain the cocktail may delay your pleasure briefly, but as Will says, the more difficult the task, the sweeter the victory.

1½fl oz/40ml vodka

2 tsp/10ml Cointreau

2 tsp/10ml apricot brandy

4 tsp/20ml lemon juice

1tsp/5ml grenadine or cherry brandy

Ice

Garnish: maraschino cherry

Combine the ingredients in a cocktail shaker with some ice and shake well. Strain and serve in a coupe (or saucer-style) champagne glass or a cocktail glass. Add the grenadine or cherry brandy at the end. Garnish with a maraschino cherry to represent that midnight sun.

"You're blended alright."

Riker (to a tipsy Troi), *Star Trek: First Contact*

Flaming Sirena

What could be more romantic at the end of the day than matching the glow of the sunset with the fires of a Flaming Sirena. Based on the classic Flaming Lamborghini, this cocktail provides a magic moment whether you are watching one sun go down or two. Just like Rios's ship, this cocktail will speed you far from your troubles.

1fl oz/25ml coffee liqueur/Kahlúa

1fl oz/25ml sambuca

1fl oz/25ml blue curaçao (or cherry liqueur)

1fl oz/25ml Irish Cream

Pour the coffee liqueur and sambuca into a cocktail glass. Set up two separate shot glasses and put the curaçao in one, and the Irish cream in the other. Light the sambuca and liqueur mixture with a match and drink it in one go with a straw. Dropping in a couple of coffee beans before you light up will enhance the flavor. Use the two shots to put out the 'fire.' Enjoy!

"To say you have no choice is a failure of imagination."

Picard, 'Et In Arcadia Ego, Pt. 2,' PIC

Pike's
Mojave Mojito

Captain Pike has seen many wonders in his life, from the Time Crystals of Boreth to the singing plants of Talos IV. But the sunset over the Mojave Desert of his childhood is the sight he recalls most fondly, and this recipe evokes the same magic. Traditionally, cane sugar provides the sweetness in this Cuban highball, but we're pushing your replicators that extra digit or two for the Mojave vibe of some agave syrup.

2fl oz/50ml white rum or tequila

1 tsp/5ml agave syrup

1fl oz/25ml lime juice

6/8 mint leaves

Drop of soda

½ lime

Garnish: lime slices, mint sprig

Muddle the agave syrup, lime and soda in a tall glass. Crush the mint leaves and add. Next add the fresh lime juice, then the rum and stir. Add soda to taste, and garnish with your mint sprig and lime slices. If you have no agave or cactus syrup handy, sugar syrup will replace happily. Serve with crushed ice for that sandy crunch.

"Be bold. Be brave. Be courageous."

Pike, 'New Eden,' DSC

"One Samarian Sunset. Made in the traditional style."

Data, 'Conundrum,' TNG

Samarian

Sunset

1½ fl oz/40ml tequila

2fl oz/50ml orange juice

2 tsp/10ml lime juice

2 tsp/10ml melon or green fruit liqueur (like banana) or blue curaçao

1 tsp/5ml of grenadine

A beautiful sunset changes a dull day into a cause for celebration, and this 24th-century concoction celebrates that feeling of transformation. There is a certain technical skill, combined with a sense of theater, in this drink that makes it the party piece of those who master it. Data has to make one for Deanna Troi, as a forfeit for losing at chess. Quark uses one in an attempt to melt the frosty heart of an ex-lover. Of course, sometimes even a sunset isn't enough. It might take a couple...

Fill a glass with ice, then add – in this order – the tequila, orange juice, and lime juice. Stir. Then add the melon or green fruit liqueur or curaçao. Finally add the grenadine without stirring, giving a light purple color.

"Behold. A gateway to your own past, if you wish."

The Guardian of Forever, 'The City on the Edge of Forever,' TOS

The Sherry On
The Edge of Forever

2fl oz/50ml dry sherry

1fl oz/25ml maraschino liqueur

Two or more orange slices

Optional 1tsp/5ml simple syrup, if you have a sweet tooth

Ice

Garnish: berries, lemon or orange wheel, mint

Behold! The Guardian of Forever is ready to take you back in time to the age of leisured drinking in the mid-nineteenth century, when the likes of Charles Dickens fell in love with the Sherry Cobbler. By adding liqueur, syrup, orange slices, and perhaps summer berries to sherry poured over crushed ice, you can influence the course of your own personal history to a pleasurable degree. Before our sun burned hot in space, someone, somewhere in the universe was enjoying a cobbler, and now you can enjoy this timeless drink, too.

Place the orange slices and syrup in a cocktail shaker and muddle. Add the sherry, maraschino liqueur, and ice, and shake very well. Strain into a tall glass or sangria-type wine glass, add plenty of crushed ice, and garnish.

We'll Always Have Paris

PICARD: I've been away far too long.

EDOUARD: Some wine,
some cheese?

PICARD: I'm not very hungry.
I really came for the view.

EDOUARD: Perhaps what you
hunger for is not on the menu.

PICARD: Perhaps not. It was many
years ago, I had a rendezvous. I was
to meet someone. Someone here,
at this very table.

EDOUARD: Your young lady,
she did not come?

PICARD: Actually, I don't know.
I always imagined that she did.

EDOUARD: You, however, did not.
Ah. Well, trust Edouard. I will bring
something very special, just for you.

Index

Cocktail recipes are highlighted in bold.

M

O

P

S

KEY

DS9 – *Star Trek: Deep Space Nine*
DSC – *Star Trek: Discovery*
ENT – *Star Trek: Enterprise*
PIC – *Star Trek: Picard*
Star Trek – the original *Star Trek* series or the franchise
TNG – *Star Trek: The Next Generation*
TOS – the original *Star Trek* series
VOY – *Star Trek: Voyager*

Go Boldly. Drink Responsibly.
GOVERNMENT WARNING: (1) According to the Surgeon General, women should not drink alcoholic beverages during pregnancy because of the risk of birth defects. (2) Consumption of alcoholic beverages impairs your ability to drive a car or operate machinery, and may cause health problems.

For further information please visit drinkaware.co.uk.

This book contains some recipes made with raw eggs. These have health risks and may cause Salmonella food poisoning so they should be treated with caution. It is prudent for vulnerable people such as pregnant and nursing mothers, invalids and the elderly to avoid these recipes. For further information visit foodsafety.gov

This book included recipes made with nuts and nut derivatives. It is advisable for those with known allergic reactions to nuts and nut derivatives to avoid these recipes.

It is also prudent to check the labels of pre-prepared ingredients for the possible inclusion of nut derivatives.

Star Trek Cocktails: A Stellar Compendium
ISBN: 9781835413913

Published by
Titan Books
A division of Titan Publishing Group Ltd
144 Southwark St
London
SE1 0UP

www.titanbooks.com

First edition: November 2024
10 9 8 7 6 5 4 3 2 1

First published by Hero Collector Books, a division of Eaglemoss Publications Ltd November 2020.
Project Concept & Management **Stella Bradley**
Designed by **Paul Montague**
Consultant **Ben Robinson**
Proofread by **Alice Peebles**

Special Thanks to **Risa Kessler and John Van Citters.**

Did you enjoy this book? We love to hear from our readers. Please e-mail us at: readerfeedback@titanemail.com or write to Reader Feedback at the above address.

To receive advance information, news, competitions, and exclusive offers online, please sign up for the Titan newsletter on our website: www.titanbooks.com

A CIP catalogue record for this title is available from the British Library.

Printed and bound in Italy.